Civic Skills and Values

# Listening

By Connor Stratton

**www.littlebluehousebooks.com**

Copyright © 2024 by Little Blue House, Mendota Heights, MN 55120. All rights reserved. No part of this book may be reproduced or utilized in any form or by any means without written permission from the publisher.

Little Blue House is distributed by North Star Editions:
sales@northstareditions.com | 888-417-0195

Produced for Little Blue House by Red Line Editorial.

Photographs ©: Shutterstock Images, cover, 4, 7, 11, 12 (top), 12 (bottom), 15 (top), 15 (bottom), 17, 20, 23, 24 (top left), 24 (top right), 24 (bottom right); iStockphoto, 9, 18–19, 24 (bottom left)

**Library of Congress Control Number: 2022919837**

**ISBN**
978-1-64619-818-4 (hardcover)
978-1-64619-847-4 (paperback)
978-1-64619-903-7 (ebook pdf)
978-1-64619-876-4 (hosted ebook)

Printed in the United States of America
Mankato, MN
082023

## About the Author

Connor Stratton writes and edits nonfiction children's books. He lives in Minnesota.

# Table of Contents

Listen and Learn  **5**

Struggles  **13**

Why It Matters  **21**

Glossary  **24**

Index  **24**

# Listen and Learn

Listening is about paying attention. You pay attention to what people say.

Listening can help you learn.

You learn new facts.

Listening can help you follow directions.

You know what to do.

Listening can help you talk to people.

You hear what they say.

When they are done speaking, you can answer.

# Struggles

Sometimes it is hard to listen.

You might feel tired.

Or you might have lots of energy.

Big feelings can make listening hard.
You might feel angry or sad.

Some things can help.
Fidget toys can help you stay calm.
Then you can focus on listening.

Making eye contact can help.

Asking questions can help too.

# Why It Matters

Listening is important.

It shows that you care.

Listening can help you connect with people. You can listen to each other.

# Glossary

**angry**

**fidget toys**

**eye contact**

**tired**

# Index

**D**
directions, 8

**F**
facts, 6

**Q**
questions, 18

**S**
sad, 14